Tell Me About You: Grandfather

By

D. Rackley

Introduction

This book is for all those questions I might not have the answers to and the questions I might not have asked. I want to build a greater understanding between us, and have a keepsake of your mind and memories. There are a few rules I would like you to follow so we can both get the most out of this book. They are as follows:

1) Be deliberate.

Please don't feel like you need to rush and answer (unless time permits). Think of what your answer might be like and ponder it. This is an exercise for you as well as to allow me to get know you on a deeper level.

2) Give as much detail as possible.

I'd appreciate as much detail as possible; I would love to know the ins and outs of your thoughts/memories. Please don't be short on your answers, as some of these questions may never come up between us again.

3) Don't hold back.

Don't feel like you can't reveal some information for one reason or another. All questions are to be answered as honestly as possible as not to insult your own memory and thoughts. Try to answer all the questions (and give a response even in the irrelevant ones) as best you can.

4) Give the book back within one year.

A time limit is to make sure you are giving answers consistent to your state of mind in this very moment. Over many years, your memory may fade more or your viewpoints on life and its circumstances may change considerably.

5) Have fun.

The most important rule is to have fun. Enjoy this book as you relive your life and ponder the world. I can't wait to get it back and read it. The more you enjoy the process, the more I will be able to see it in your writing. Feel free to customise this book to your liking, draw in the corners and make it your own if you wish. This book is a piece of you.

Ready? Here it begins. Let's start at the beginning...

Childhood

Childhood (0-12 years)

Introduction to life

What's the story of your birth?

What's the story of your name?

What is your earliest childhood memory?

Describe your living circumstances as a child?

Relationships with others

What was your relationship with your parents like growing up?

What are some of the most important lessons you learned from your parents?

What was your relationship with your grandparents like growing up?

What are some important lessons you learned from your grandparents?

What was something you learned from interacting with people outside your immediate family?

What was your relationship like with your sibling/s?

Which family member were you closest to? Why?

Who were your childhood best friends/companions?

Who had the biggest impact on your personality?

Child's Mind

What were some childhood dreams/aspirations you had?

What were some of the hardest moments you experienced as a child?

What did you want to do for a living as a child? Why?

What were you most scared of?

What didn't make sense to you as much as you tried to understand it?

Interactions with the world

What were your favourite things to do as a child?

Where was your favourite place to go as a child?

Did you ever break any rules? If so, what did you do?

What was your favourite childhood movie? Why?

What talents were you most gifted among your peers with?

What was your favourite music to listen to as a child?

Reflection

What was a major turning point in your childhood? Why?

Did any major world events affect you as a child? If so, how?

Is there anything that you missed out on as a child?

If you could have said anything to your adult self, what would you have said?

If you could speak to your child self now, what would you say?

What would you have changed about your childhood if you could?

When did you know you had crossed into adolescence?

Adolescence & Young Adulthood

Adolescence & Young Adulthood (12-21)

<u>Shaping your personality</u>

Who had the most influence on you?

What experience had the most influence on you?

What piece of media (ie. book, radio broadcast, tv show, music) had the most influence on you? Why?

Who did you go to for advice growing up? In hindsight, were they correct or wrong?

The Adolescent Experience

What was some of your favourite music?

Tell me a funny story that you still laugh about today

What are you proud to have accomplished growing up?

What were your usual weekends like?

Is there anything that you feel hasn't changed between our adolescence?

What's an embarrassing thing/moment your mum or dad did to you?

What's your opinion on your hometown?

Your early life firsts

What's the first album you ever bought? Do you still listen to them?

Who was your first kiss? What was the story?

Where was your first trip to without your immediate family? Tell me about it

What was your first major purchase? Why'd you spend it on that?

Where was your first job? Tell me about it

Shaping your life

What did you envision for your adulthood at this stage?

Did any world events affect your adolescence? If so, how?

Did you cut any friends from your circle? If so, why?

What's the dumbest thing you did as an adolescent? What did you learn?

What is something that felt right at the time, but turned out to be a mistake?

Do you have any regrets during this time? If so, how would things have been different if you did/didn't do them?

When did you know you crossed into adulthood?

Adulthood

Adulthood (21+)

Relationships, Things & Experiences

How did you meet my grandmother?

In your opinion, what is essential to a successful relationship/marriage?

Tell me about your relationship with your parents during adulthood

How did your relationship change with your parents over time?

What was something you threw away that you wish you had today?

What is your favourite movie? Why?

Who is your favourite musician/band? Why?

What is the most memorable lesson you learned from your parents? How has it helped you?

What trait did you admire most about your mum/and or dad?

Which parent were you closest to? Why?

In what ways had your parents let you down?

What is one of your favourite memories of being a dad?

What has been the best book you have ever read?

What's the best gift you've ever received?

What's the best gift you've ever given?

Best place you have ever travelled to? Why?

Places you would like to visit but have not yet?

Adult Life

What has been the best thing about being an adult?

What is the hardest thing about being an adult?

What accomplishment are you most proud of?

What are some of the most amazing things you have experienced?

What is something you look forward to every day?

What was the best live event that you went to?

What is your most embarrassing moment?

What were the biggest turning points of your adulthood? Why?

What are some habits that you wish you could kick? Why can't you?

What are some habits that you're thankful you have?

What would you consider to be your best personality trait?

Have you ever used any illegal drugs?

What is your dream job?

What has been the greatest day of your life so far?

The Adult Mind

What is your definition of the 'meaning of life'?

Did you end up where you thought you'd be?

What do you know is an absolute fact?

If you could have dinner with 3 people (dead or alive) who would it be and why?

What have you taken for granted?

What was/is the greatest personal obstacle in your life? How did you overcome it or learned to manage it?

What are some of the hardest things you have ever had to do?

What is your biggest worry at the moment? Why?

What is your greatest fear in life? Why?

Have any world events affected you as an adult? If so, how?

Has your life been affected by a war? If so, what happened?

Do you consider yourself to be successful?

What are some of your goals for the future?

What memory instantly makes you smile?

What would you consider to be your most useful talent/personality trait?

What is a quote that you live by?

Do you have any unconventional advice that has worked for you?

What are the best pieces of advice you ever received?

What would be the soundtrack of your life? Why?

Philosophical Thoughts

Philosophical Thoughts

What do you believe happens when we die?

If you had 100 million dollars, how would you spend it?

Have you ever experienced anything paranormal?

Do you believe the world is good/bad or just has both elements in it?

What do you believe we were before our birth?

What do you think is essential to have to live a happy life?

Are you a product of your environment or born the way you are?

Do you believe there is life on another planet?

What is the most important trait someone can have?

What would make the world a better place?

Can you have happiness without sadness?

What is love?

If you are born again, what animal would you like to be?

If you are born again, what country would you like it to be?

Is suffering part of the human condition? Does hardship make people stronger?

How do you deal with stress?

What's a social or political cause you're most passionate about? Was there another one before?

What are your political views? How do you think they were formed?

How would you describe your relationship with money?

If you could rid the world of one thing, what would it be? Why?

About Us

About Us

Tell me something random about you that I would not know

What's something you wish you could have told me growing up but couldn't? Why?

Is there anything in our family that you've kept a secret?

What has been the best gift I have ever given you?

What did I do growing up that frustrated you?

What did I do growing up that made you laugh?

What do I do now that makes you laugh?

When was the first time you heard me swear?

What song reminds you of me most?

When have I cheered you up without knowing it at the time?

When have I made you upset without knowing it at the time?

How are we similar?

How are we different?

How could things be better between us?

What's a common value/trait in our family that you disagree with?

What is our strongest asset as a family?

What do I do that makes you upset? Why?

What do I do that makes you happy? Why?

What's the worst fight that we have had? Why?

What is your proudest moment of me?

What did you think I would be when I grew up?

What is a piece of advice you have for my life?

Where should I look for you when you're not around?

What is your hope for me?

What is your favourite moment of us together?

Conclusion & Thankyou

Conclusion

There is just one thing left to do in this book. I would like you to leave me a surprise in this book or give a priceless gift when you return the book back to me. Just for some ideas, it could be a photo of us that you love, a small sentimental item, an old keepsake etc.

Thank you for spending your time answering my questions, I believe this will be a book that I cherish forever. I love you.

www.ingramcontent.com/pod-product-compliance
Ingram Content Group UK Ltd.
Pitfield, Milton Keynes, MK11 3LW, UK
UKHW020424250726
13967UKWH00007B/2796